A Pictorial American River Bike Trail Trip
From Old Sacramento to Folsom Lake
By Steve Holmes

If you go online to "American River Bike Trail (Jedediah Smith Memorial Trail) you can download a PDF file with the above picture of the whole trail. There is also a web site for the trail:
http://www.americanriverbiketrail.com

Though it was recognized as a national trail in 1974, I started to ride before then since it wasn't too far from where I lived. When I first rode on it, it went from Discovery Park to just over the levee at Rio Americano High School, which is around mile 11.7 on the trail now. It now starts in Old Sacramento and to get to mile 0.0 in Discovery Park, it's about a mile away. Mile point 31 is just a tenth of a mile or so before you get to Beals Point. I have personally logged thousands of miles on the trail, both bicycling and running alongside it. (Many people run alongside it. Much of it has decomposed granite next to it but some spots don't have good enough shoulders for the granite so runners tend to run on the asphalt.

It includes 450 feet of elevation according to the local sources, traveling 32 miles from Old Sacramento to Beals Point at Folsom Lake with mileage markers at half mile points up to mile 22.5 but not so well marked after that. There is a yellow line down the middle with space enough for two bicycles to comfortably (and safely) ride next to one another. The terrain is mostly flat with a few minor hills with a bigger hill at the end to get to the top of the lake's levee. If you take the northern route around Lake Natoma, just a little downstream from Folsom, there are a couple of steeper hills.

Getting back to "safety", there are many cyclists who ride fast on the trail for their workouts. The official speed limit is 15 mph and for a few days in the summer of 2014 there were rangers out there with radar guns to warn faster riders, but it seems it was a losing battle to regulate the riders' speed.

Every cyclist should be prepared in case of an emergency. First of all, wear a helmet. Though I had one on at the time of my last accident on the trail where I was only going the 15 mph speed limit, a squirrel tried to jump through the spokes of my front wheel, made it only half way, jammed my front wheel to a stop, and I awoke in the hospital. Second of all, have a pump for your particular type of tube (Presta or Schraeder), two spare tubes so you can quickly swap a good one for a punctured one twice, and a tube repair kit (which includes tire irons) if you are so unfortunate to have more than two flats.

Of those racers, many go in groups. Groups tend to be three to five riders but there are occasionally larger groups. There are a few cycling groups around town. Two old and big ones are Sacramento Bike Hikers and the Sacramento Wheelmen.

On the other end of the scale, there are little kids on tiny bikes, runners pushing kids in strollers, and skating is also legal on the trail. Skateboards are illegal, as are motor bikes, but I have seen them.

Anyhow, as all my miles on the trail attest, the American River Bike Trail is a great resource for Sacramento County. When I left to work jobs elsewhere for ten years, it was the trail that made me decide that I wanted to settle down within a few miles of the trail to live.

If you come from the goldish Tower Bridge, there is a sign to direct you to Old Sacramento

There is a nice exhibit of old train cars to the left, by the old train station replica. The brick buildings have nice exhibits and school children pan for gold in front of them.

This is the street nearest to the Freeway. It's hard to find parking on the old street but there are parking lots nearby.

To get to the actual start of the trail, head past those trees on the far left to the river.

There are at least two bike rental shops in Old Sacramento. One is open year round and also sells electric-powered bikes. The other one was operating during the summer near the old train station and it rented all kinds of bike: clunkers, tandems, and even quadricycles.

One of the attractions of Old Sacramento is the old train rides that can be taken down the river in the summer.

The bike trail starts here. The sign shows that it is one mile to Discovery Park's Mile 0.0

Follow the river's edge up stream. Lots of downtown workers run along this portion of the trail during their lunch time.

On the right side of the trail, past the freeway, is the old railyard. A bit further on the trail you'll come across this artistic water display.

Down the trail a bit, you'll see the confluence of the
Sacramento River and the American River. Up ahead is a
green bridge to cross over to get to Discovery Park.

Down the hill from the green bridge, take a left turn to get on the
bike trail. Then follow it around under the bridge to get to mile 0.0

A number of homeless people can frequently be seen in Discovery Park. They make homes along the trail for the first couple of miles, too. Some cyclists have been accosted on the trail on rare occasions but the trail is considered safe overall.

You'll pass an archery range on the left and then swing right to ride beneath a canopy of trees that can be a nice relief from a hot summer sun.

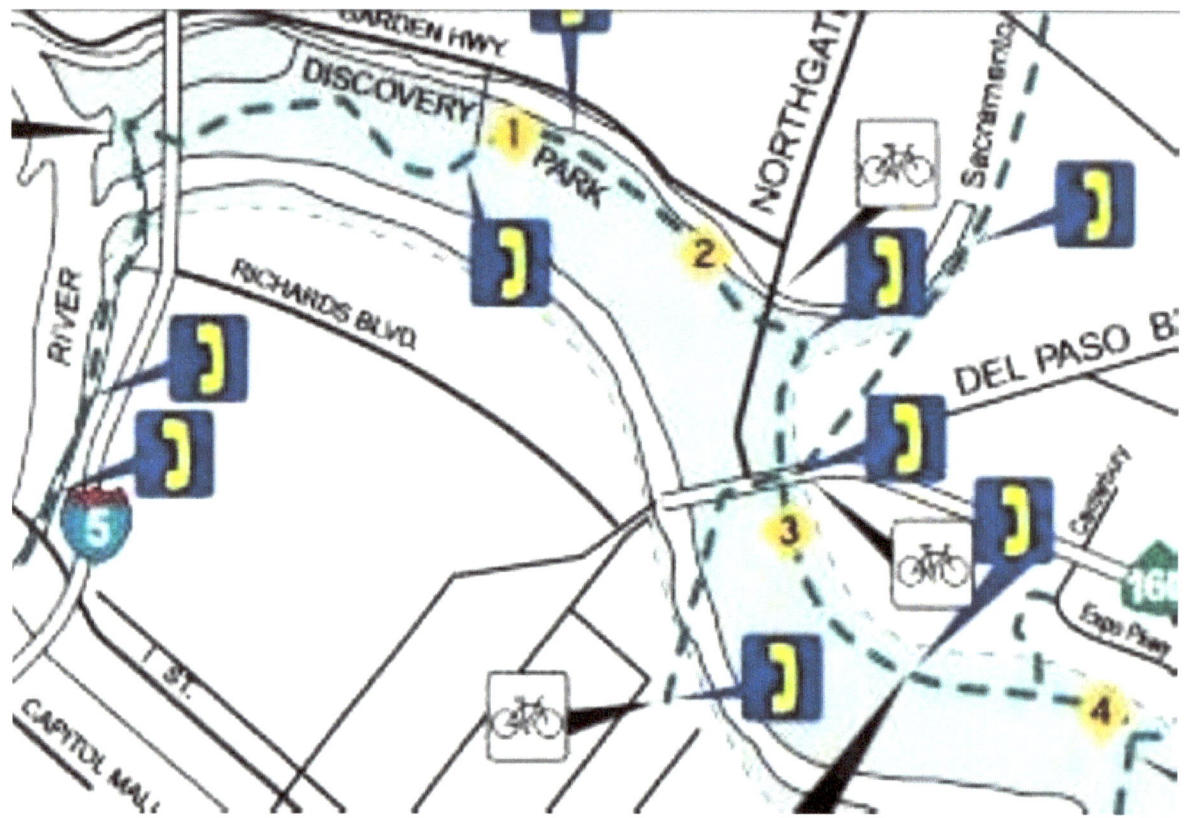

On this piece of the official bike trail map, shown above, you can see where there are emergency phones and see the mile markers. I noticed that the emergency phones at miles 1 and 2 were gone, though.

You might have noticed some sort of waterway between the bike trail and the levee on the left. Here near Mile 3 is a good view of it. It was created because soil was needed to create the levee.

There are frequently fires along the bike trail, especially near Discovery Park.

As the map of the trail shows, there emergency phones at regular intervals, though the ones at Mile 1 and Mile 2 were vandalized.

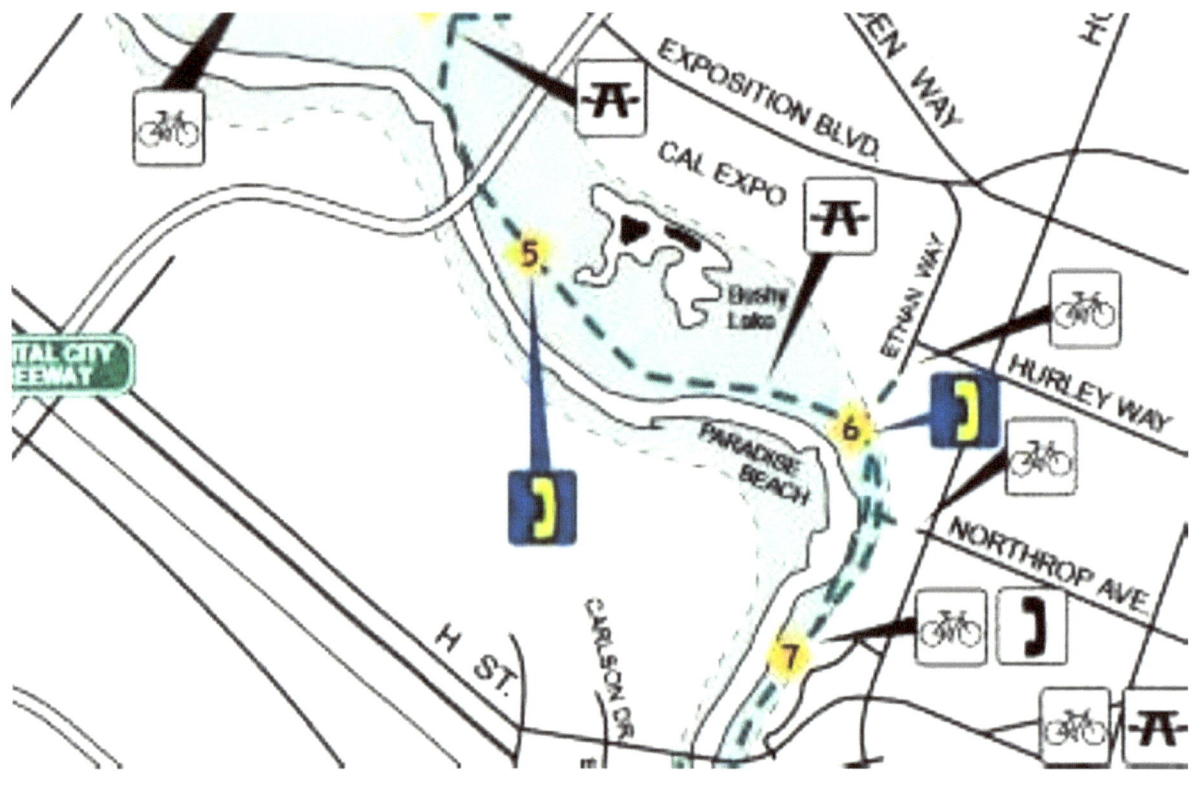

Off to the left side of the trail, past Bush Lake, is the white Cal Expo water tower.

Here, at Mile 6, there is this plaque by the turnoff to Cal Expo

Up toward Mile 7 is this short golf course on the right side.

Mile 8 is a little beyond Guy West Bridge, seen here. It joins college student residences on the left with the college on the right. It's hard to see but this is one of three bike repair stations with a pump and

Many runners or cyclists meet up at the Guy West Bridge for some exercise. If you happen to be at this spot in the middle of July, you will see thousands of bicycles set up for participants of Eppie's Great Race, the world's oldest triathlon. The trail from here to mile 20 is closed that morning because of the race.

There is an alternate bike trail leg on the south side of the river that you can get to by crossing the Guy West Bridge and turning left on the levee.

Here is a tunnel of trees on the south side leg of the bike trail.

On that south side route, which isn't very long, is "University Grove", a lawn area near the college. At the end of that segment, you need to cross over the river to return to the main bike trail.

Here, still on the south side leg near Mile 10 there, is a parking lot and restroom to make it convenient to start/end there.

Back on the northern leg of the trail, here is a well-used rest stop with a drinking fountain for runners or cyclists just past Mile 9

Here is a view of the Watt Ave bridge, which is another place where people frequently start and end their adventures. That structure is a restroom and there's a drinking fountain, too.

Just past Mile 10 is a spot where I frequently see male turkeys trying to attract the ladies in the spring.

A little before Mile 11 is another tunnel of trees that I always enjoy.

Several memorial benches have been put here and there along the bike train in shady spots for taking a break, like this one before Mile 11

At this spot before Mile 12 is a place to see waterfowl in the river inlet. This is near where the bike trail used to end, with Rio American High School over the levee to the left.

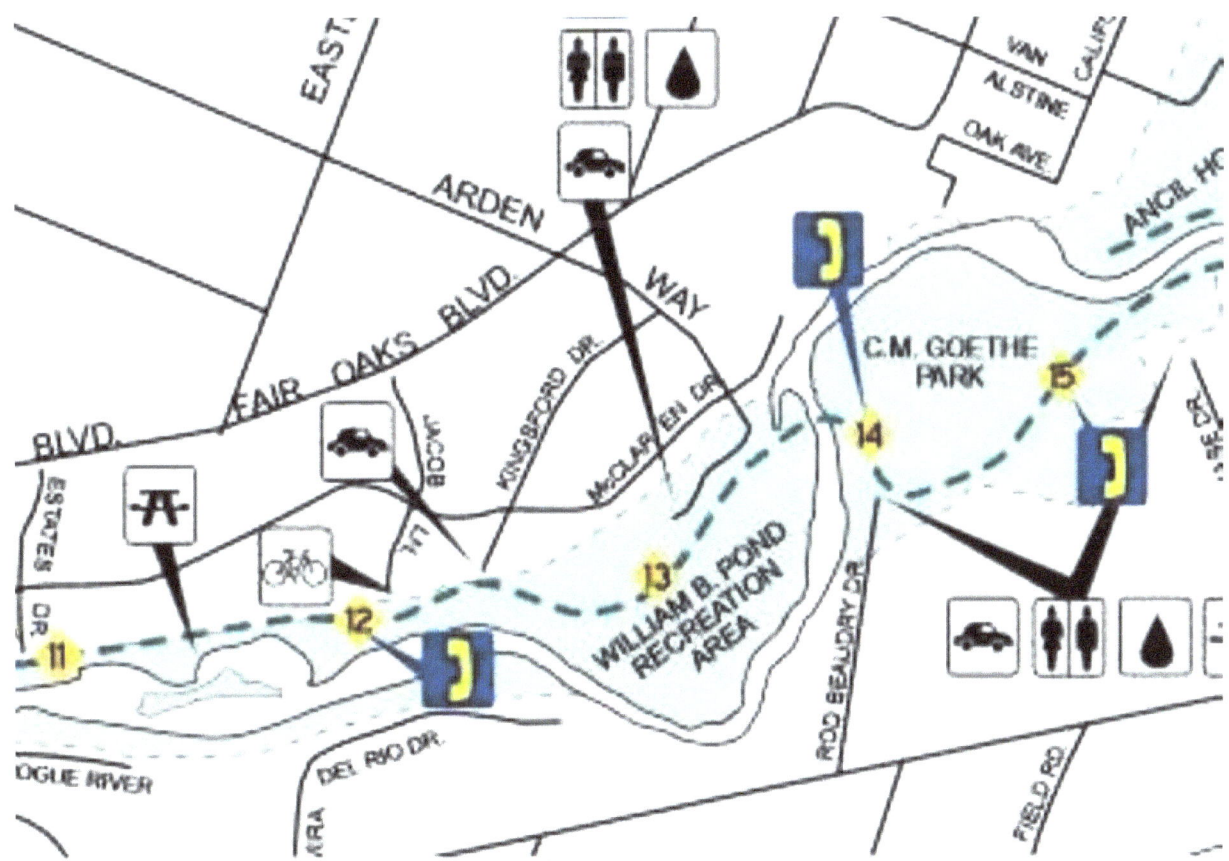

William Pond Recreation Area and River Bend Park (formerly known as Goethe Park) are a couple of good spots to reach the trail. The start of Eppie's Great Race is at Mile 12.5 in the middle of July.

Memorial to Eppie Johnson, creator of Eppie's Great Race, at the start of the race at Mile 12.5

The race has become a big part of what happens in Sacramento. Eppie died not long after the 40th race in 2013. There are thousands of volunteers who help with the event each year. If you are in Sacramento on the weekend of the race, it's a sight to behold.

Here is a view from the Harold Richey bridge that goes over the river between William Pond and River Bend parks when the kayaks from the Eppie's Great Race particpants have finished the race.

There is a slight hill to Mile 15 where to the right is a project to grow trees to revegetate the river area

A little past the tree growing area is a little bridge and right after that is a sign that tells of a little farm off in the background on the right side. On weekends during growing season, there is a sign out advertising the crops for sale at the upcoming Cordova Park.

Here you see the west end of the Cordova Park with the enclosed area for dogs. At the east end of the park is a mini-train track that rides are given on.

On the left side of the trail, a little past Mile 17, is another spot where I usually see male turkeys trying to woo females in the spring.

Here is a bench right before a little hill to Mile 17.5 where you start to see lots of rocks piled up from after the gold rush

Starting in the spring there are many black caterpillers with bright orange spots on them. Those caterpillers live on the Dutchman's pipe vine. Soon afterward, there are many butterflies all about that are black with metallic blue on them.

Here is the actual Dutchman's Pipe flower but they're hard to spot because they come out early in the year and are greenish.

Here just past Mile 18, on the left side of the trail, is a plaque to commemorate the trail.

There are other plaques along the trail and there was one right across from Mile 18, too, near the table that had the Pipe Vine all covered with the caterpillars.

Here is my favorite tunnel of trees near Mile 18.5. There is a small park there but the drinking fountain hasn't been functional for a long time.

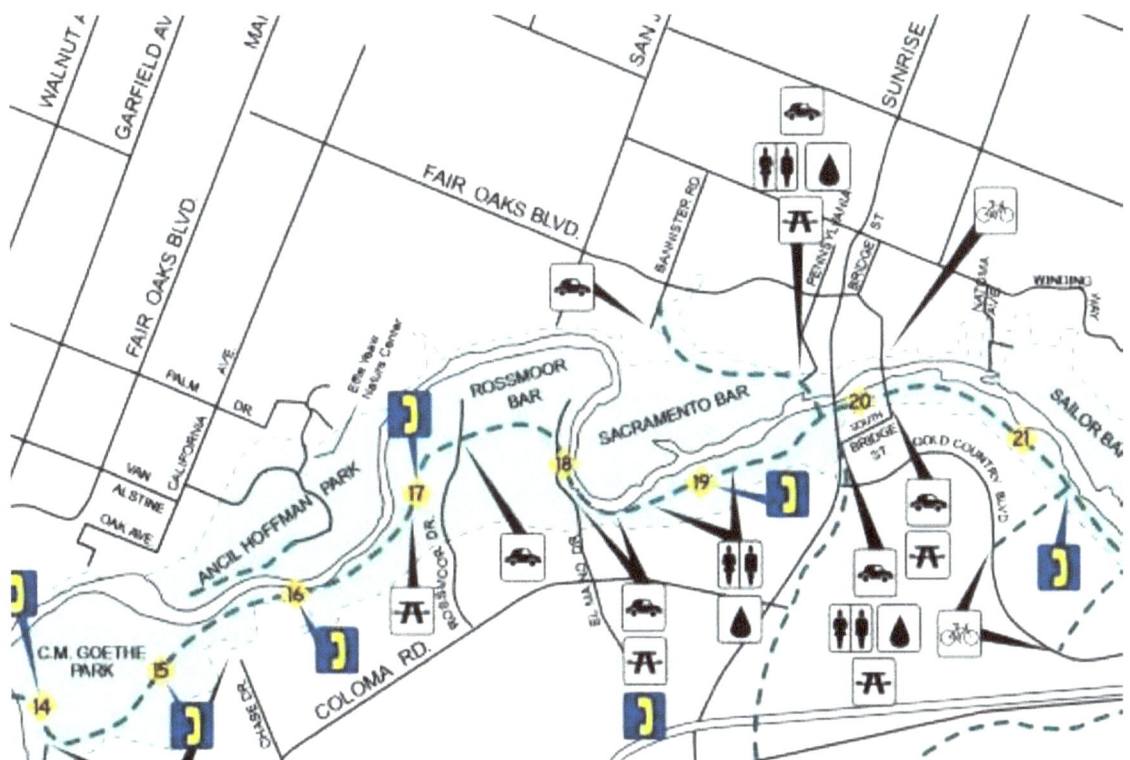

Here is the official map of the last stretch of the trail.

Here is a park a little past Mile 19, where I have again seen male turkeys trying to attract females in the spring. This is a fairly popular park to stop at by cyclists and runners due to the restroom and drinking fountain there

This is the "lower Sunrise parking lot" after Mile 19.5. There used to be stop signs for cyclists whereever there were road crossings but cyclists tended not to stop for them so they were mostly eliminated, except for ones like here.

This is where the cycling portion of Eppie's Great Race ends. After hopping off one's bike, the racer runs across the old bridge, through a tunnel of other relay racers to then paddle to the finish back at River Bend (Goethe) Park

Here is the Nimbus Fish Hatchery at Mile 22.5. It is a fun place to visit in the fall when the salmon are going up the fish ladder. This is another popular place for cyclists and runners to start/end their trail adventure.

At the fish hatchery you have to make a choice as to which way to proceed past Lake Natoma. I like to go counter-clockwise, but for no special reason. To do that, I cross Hazel Avenue at the light, proceed toward the Aquatic Center, but right before getting to the parking lot I take a right turn on to the trail. If I were to go the other way around Lake Natoma, I would ride on the sidewalk on the left side to the top of the Hazel Avenue Bridge, take a sharp left turn on to the trail there, follow the trail back under Hazel Avenue, and be on my way. In either case, the miles aren't as well marked as earlier on the trail.

Near Mile 28 or so you can look across Lake Natoma to the cliffs on the other side.

Here near mile 26.9 on the north side of Lake Natoma is an info spot that tells about the local geology

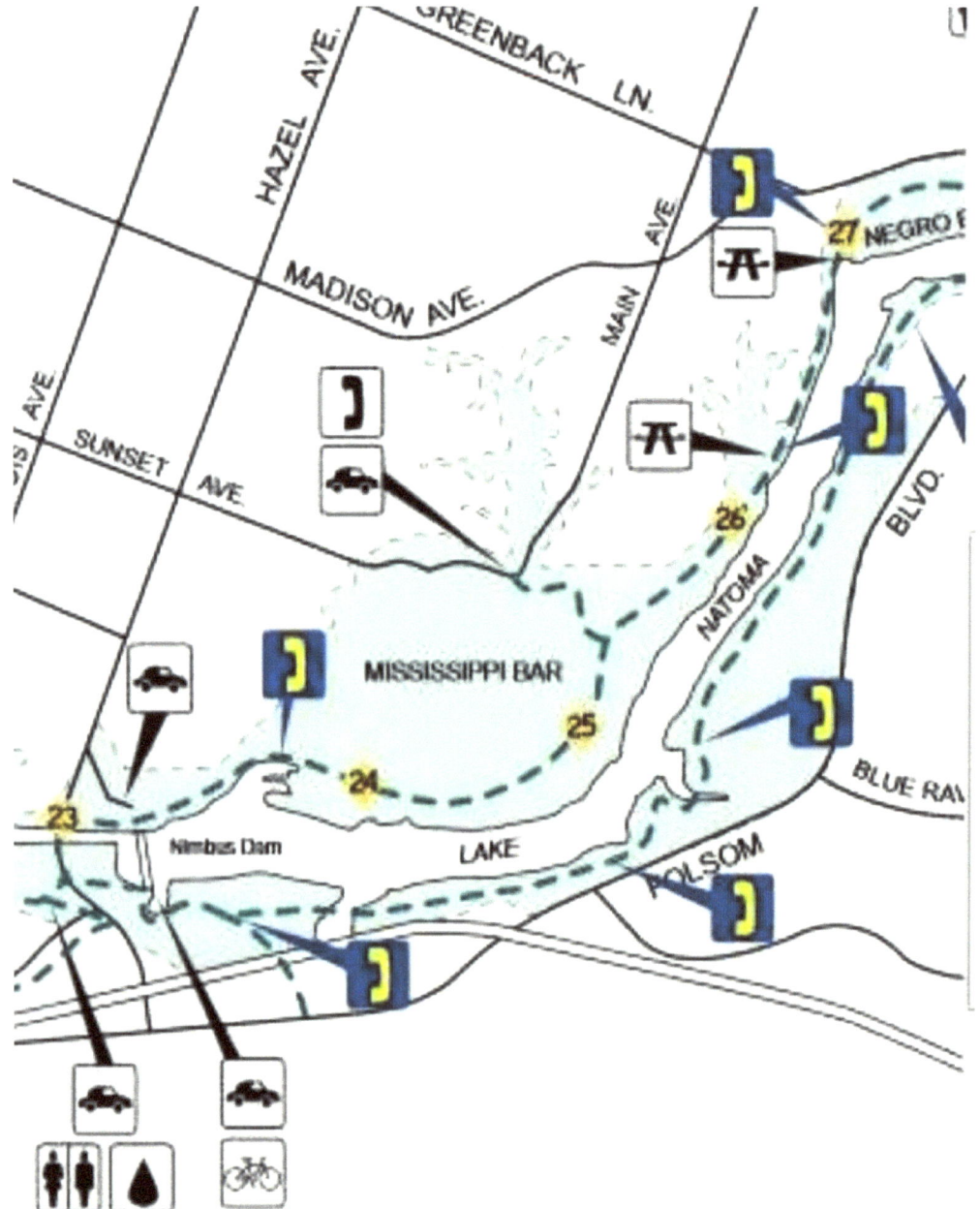

Here is another section of the official bike route map, which shows the route on both sides of Lake Natoma

When you get to Folsom on the trail, it's a bit tricky to follow it. You will ride under the new Rainbow Bridge and then soon after there will be a little offshoot that is hardly noticeable but you should take it. It leads to the back of a hotel so if you don't see the hotel right there, you aren't at the correct spot. Anyhow, take an immediate right turn in the parking lot, go up the hill that winds to the left, going past a restaurant and a bike shop, turn left on that road immediately in front of you, follow the road to the stop light, turn left at the stop light, get to another stop light pretty fast, and just past that stop light the bike trail continues next to the road that goes over the old Rainbow Bridge. You might see a park at the old Folsom Powerhouse across the road to the left right there, too.

Head down that slight hill to the old metal bridge (there's some interesting history for that bridge) and to go to Beals Point take a right turn at the "T" intersection just past that old metal bridge. Get ready for a fairly steep climb through a nice wooded area and it's roughly one mile to Beals Point.

After you go under a little residential area bridge, there is this old rock building on the left side. There once was info about it but that info is no longer there. On the right side of the trail is an abandoned olive orchard and old rusted pump hidden away.

Upon reaching the top of that hill, you will find Beals Point on the right. In the summer there is a snack bar there. For the adventurous, you can follow the road atop the levee. At the end of that piece of the levee is a rough dirt trail that goes to Cavitt School, near Granite Bay. It's popular to drive to Cavitt School to begin a mountain bike ride over the hilly dirt trails to Granite Bay State Park. On the other side of Granite Bay Park the dirt trail continues and there is a hill that is fun to ride a mountain bike up to get a hilltop view of the lake. From there, the trail winds around the hill and takes you back to the trail from Granite Bay.

If interested in mountain bike riding, there are more trails in the vicinity of Folsom Lake. One trail is at the Salmon Falls Bridge. I won't go into detail about that because that isn't part of the American River Bike trail (yet).

This is a panoramic view of Folsom Lake from the levee just past Beals Point (about Mile 31.2) in October, 2014. I grew up near there and the lake had so much water in the lake that it almost drowned out Beals Point.

The ride down from Beals Point is a fun fast one but after that residential bridge it's best to use caution. Not far past where a sign tells you you're at Mile 30 is a view of Folsom Prison, across the river.

Getting back toward Hazel Avenue, you might see thousands of birds on the lake or maybe you'll see the college rowing teams with their white tents.

It's somewhat common to see deer on the bike trail.

Here are a few of the critters on the trail. It's not often for me to see a coyote. Some years back, there was a momma coyote and two youngsters. In the last years I see coyotes from Mile 9 to Mile 19. I have a suspicion that this is two different coyotes instead of one doing that much wandering mainly because that area includes both sides of the river.

Mountain lions have been seen on the trail and even in East Sacramento but that is extremely rare.

Did you see any of these critters?

Don't get freaked out by a rattle snake. As with lizards, they are frequently just trying to stay warm on the asphalt. No, they can't jump out at you. They can strike out half the length of their body. It's best to just scare them off the trail before they (not you) get hurt.

Coyote a bit before Mile 18.5

These critters are out more on the trail as the air isn't warm enough for them so they lie on the trail to get warm (please don't run them over)

Though there is an alternative choice back to downtown Sacramento that you can take near Mile 3, I don't recommend it. Now and then I've seen large groups of homeless people just around that corner.

If you did the whole 65 mile round trip from Old Sacramento to Beals Point and back, this view of Discovery Park might be quite welcome. Treat yourself to some dessert in Old Sacramento as a reward for your effort!

www.ingramcontent.com/pod-product-compliance
Lightning Source LLC
Chambersburg PA
CBHW060815290526
45792CB00005BB/1669